# *WHEN THE BALL IS LAID TO REST*

# WHEN THE BALL IS LAID TO REST

**Poetry and Prose by Adonal Foyle**

*Adonal Foyle*

Copyright © 2017 Adonal Foyle Enterprises

All rights reserved. No part of this book may be reproduced, stored, or transmitted by any means whether auditory, graphic, mechanical, or electronic without written permission of both publisher and author, except in the case of brief excerpts used in critical articles and reviews. Unauthorized reproduction of any part of this work is illegal and is punishable by law.

ISBN 13: 978-1-944-662-50-9

Published by Realization Press

Cover Design by MASgraphicarts.com

# Table of Contents

*Introduction* ............................................................... *xii*
**Foreword** ................................................................. xiv
Dedication ................................................................. xvi
*Acknowledgements* ................................................ *xviii*

**Caribbean Life** .......................................................... 1
WHERE IN THE WORLD IS HE FROM? ................. 2
SCHOOL DAYS ........................................................ 6
SATURDAY BLUES .................................................. 7
RUNNING ................................................................ 9
QUESTIONS ........................................................... 11
SHE SAID ............................................................... 13
BEFORE THEY THROW YOU IN THE GROUND . 14
MAYPOLE DANCING ............................................ 15
DRY SEASON ......................................................... 17
ISLAND WITCH ..................................................... 19
DAMN SUN ............................................................ 20
SLIDING IN COPPER POT ................................... 22
WE TOO CAN BUILD COMPUTER CHIPS ......... 23
SWEET CHANT ..................................................... 26
A PLACE OF MYSTERY ......................................... 30
REMEMBERING THE PAST .................................. 31

**Pick and Roll** .................................................... 33
LOSING ................................................................ 34
AIR BALL ............................................................. 35
WARRIOR OF THE BAY ................................... 40
DRUMMING THE WARRIORS BACK TO LIFE ...... 38
COURT AT NIGHT .............................................. 36
JUST BUSINESS .................................................. 37
LOVE SONG TO A GAME ................................. 42

**Politics** ............................................................. 45
BENEATH THE WAVING FLAG ........................ 46
THE KING OF HIS TIME ..................................... 49
GLORY ................................................................. 50

**A Love Story** ................................................... 51
BREAKFAST AT CHOWS .................................... 52
NIGHT AND DAY: A LOVE POEM .................... 54
LOVE ON A TRAIN ............................................ 57

**Glossary Of Caribbean Terms** ...................... 65
**About The Author** .......................................... 69

# *Introduction*

Beginning in high school, poetry has played an important role in my life. I started writing for my AP English class. Since then poetry lines dance in my head, forcing this language of expression to frame a thought or a moment that I cannot explain with conventional language. When I went to college, I had the opportunity to work with Peter Balakian. He was my professor at Colgate University and he really helped me nurture my true love for poetry.

One day I got a call from Professor Balakian asking me to come back and read some of my poems to his class. It caused me to go back through most of the poetry I had written over the years. I decided to put a series of poems together to present to the class and I thought this could also be the way to present my first book of poetry to the world.

This book contains samples of everything I have written over the years. I have tried to show the range and diversity of my poetry, and I hope everyone gets a chance to see the different sides of me through my poems.

I have always felt that writing my thoughts down in poetry form has helped me to express my concerns and feelings that were otherwise difficult to voice. For example, when I graduated from college and when I retired from the NBA, I wrote poems as a way to say farewell. Whenever there have been big moments in my life such as the death of my grandmother, death of a dear friend, a

*Adonal Foyle*

wedding, or a moment of clarity, I have always used poetry to mark the occasion.

Writing poetry has been a way to tell my stories in a controlled and yet poignant way. It is where I can pour out my soul. It has always been an outlet for me and very personal. Publishing my poems is a new departure for me. I am at a point however where I am comfortable sharing this side of myself. I hope you enjoy reading them.

Adonal D. Foyle

# *Foreword*

Every teacher of writing has moments that stay with him. Moments when students do special things, when students write something that's a leap forward, a lovely rich surprise. One of those moments happened for me in the spring of 1997 when I was teaching my poetry-writing workshop at Colgate University.

That week my student Adonal Foyle was presenting his sonnet to be work-shopped by the class. When he read his poem "Island Witch," I was struck by the notes he had hit; the poem had a beautiful balance of music and image and it brought together folkloric dimensions of Adonal's Caribbean culture with a boy's memory of fear and wonder. I excerpt a stanza here:

*With salt and pepper stain the hunter's prey,*

*to burn and burn will be its deadly fate.*

*And it must turn toward the morning rays,*

*the zephyr pulls the sun onto the lake.*

Since that class Adonal has done many things. He was drafted eighth overall in the 1997 NBA draft and played power forward for the Golden State Warriors and Orlando Magic for 13 years. He has been the vice president of the NBA Players Association. He has been inducted into the World

*Adonal Foyle*

Sports Humanitarian Hall of Fame. He has been appointed goodwill ambassador for St. Vincent and the Grenadines. He has founded two humanistic non-profit groups, The Kerosene Lamp Foundation and Democracy Matters. He earned a master's degree in Sports Psychology. And more.

But through it all Adonal has written poems. For him poetry continues to be a necessary marker in his life, a fundamental way of making meaning. His poems take on a broad range of experience that include personal relationships, politics and race, life in the NBA, and his Caribbean childhood on the island of Canouan (part of St. Vincent's in the Grenadines). Adonal can write in quatrains as he does in his poem to Martin Luther King, Jr. "King of His Time," or a voodoo free verse chant as in his poem, "Bringing the Warriors Back to Life."

In Adonal's poems of childhood, like "School Days," and "Running," his sensual memories of Caribbean life collide with harsh realities of coming of age. And his poems about the present engage the ironies of post-colonial life as in, "We too can build computer chips":

> *Fishermangumboats/pulledtotheshore/hiddeninthe shade of the tuckeberry/Now we scrub/white man's floor/from seven to four for pennies.*

You'll find his passion and understanding of the game of basketball in a series of poems that consider the game in "on the court" encounters and more reflective views of the pulse of the game as a trope for life. Is there another NBA player who has ever taken on the meaning of the game in the form of lyric poems? If so, I'm unaware of him or her. Former NBA center, son of Canouan, Caribbean American poet Adonal Foyle is an original. Anyone who picks up *When the Ball is Laid to Rest* will find poems of an authentic self forever wrestling with meaning in fresh ways.

Peter Balakian,
January 2017

*Adonal Foyle*

# Dedication

I dedicate this Book to my grandmother, Faith Baptiste and my Aunt, Islar Baptiste. All you asked of me was to be a humble human being. I hear your whispers beyond the grave.

I also dedicate this book to my AP high school English teacher, Gary Rider at Hamilton High School. It was in your class I first read Shakespeare and fell in love with a sonnet. It was in your class that I wrote my first poem.

# *Acknowledgements*

Writing is a particularly daunting task for me.

Wherever I am in the world it is my first instinct to write, and I am usually not bothered by diction or structure.

It is through rewriting and having other people review my work that the work is done. To that end, there are numerous people who have helped me bring this work forward.

I would like to thank Nan Washburn, my high school English teacher, for teaching me how to conjugate a verb, how to embrace the English language, and how to make an argument on paper. Peter Balakian for truly teaching me how to find my voice and the power of the right word.

Christopher Navalta for always being willing to look over my work, providing constructive criticism, and asking me to push a little deeper. Stephen Eriksen for believing in me on a daily basis and creating the space for me to work.

My American mother, Joan Mandle, for being the first person to read my poetry from high school on, and for believing in me and my writing. Shiyana Valentine for always believing that I should share my poems with the world and for pushing me forward. And finally, Olivia Duba, for bringing a fresh pair of eyes to the project and for taking me on her new poetry journey.

# Caribbean Life

*There's definitely healing properties to being in proximity to the ocean and that breeze. There's something about that Caribbean climate and humidity.*

Johnny Depp

*Adonal Foyle*

## WHERE IN THE WORLD IS HE FROM?

I hail from a land where the river runs into the sea,

where mosquitoes are as popular as Captain Bligh's breadfruit.

A land barricaded by water like a pearl seeking refuge in the belly of a clam.

A place deep, deep in the entrails of the Caribbean Sea.

Where drums and steel pans remind us of our ancestral past.

A place where soca, reggae, dub, and

calypso expose the politics of our time.

Where Christmas is a nine-day fete

and Carnival fills July with ole mas'

and jubay mornin'.

Where curry goat and coconut water

flavor the midday air.

The heart of the Lesser Antilles,

with wongoo and okra,

bakes and salt fish our national treasures.

*When the Ball is Laid to Rest*

An island where snow refuses to fall,

and diamond beaches sparkle in

the thick of black night.

A home where donkeys plod on narrow streets.

A place where the sun finally gathers

its belongings and sinks into oblivion.

Where the moon turns night into day.

With villagers telling of Socouyant, Jabless,

Jumbies, and wicked ghosts who snatch

and devour disobedient children.

Part of an archipelago of gems forming the Windward Islands.

Where farmers work with hoes and cutlass and

everything you eat springs from the overgrown soil.

Where boys and girls brush their teeth

with ashes or sand and lotion their chocolate skin with dabs of cooking oil.

*Adonal Foyle*

Where a common cold is cured with a sip of cod liver oil

and baby spoon of whale oil.

A place where two mango

seeds and a stick yield a beautiful toy.

A place where on Saturday the island pauses

to juke their laundry in washtubs and pails.

Where school children in khaki pants and gray shirts

walk barefoot to school four times a day.

Shouts ring out as they pick cricket,

soccer, rounddodge, and netball teams at recess.

A place where boys and girls are spanked if their nails are dirty

or their hair is fray-fray or for not saying

good evening to an auntie on the street.

Where children study by

kerosene lamp and candlelight.

I am talking about a place where hibiscus,

morning glory, bougainvillea, and the blue, gold

and green flag with its V of diamonds,

dance in the cool Caribbean breeze.

Where is this land of fishermen sailing at dawn?

Searching the vast sea for Blue Tang, French Grunt,

Peacock Flounder, Yellow Tails and Goliath Grouper.

Where little boys fish on rocks

and pick Wilkes at the edge of the ocean.

St. Vincent and the Grenadines is the mother country

but Canouan, that beautiful island,

that's where I'm from.

*Adonal Foyle*

## SCHOOL DAYS

Hezachia Jones is dead,

rotting in the latrine pit.

Now Lolo Beff, the replacement wooden paddle,

makes Louis, the nutty professor, giggle.

Together they bend, discipline, humiliate.

12 X 5?

Spell "necessary"?

Extend your hands, palms up.

Late again?

Turn, bend over, clutch your knees.

Lolo Beff pays homage.

Two feet of pine, carved lovingly,

a paddle of necessity.

The jagged white surface carries its name,

my ass still carries its scars.

## SATURDAY BLUES

Under the tamarind tree Lola sits

with her juke board and washtub

scrubbing the damn clothes back to life.

The radio blares Bob Marley,

Redemption Song. It's all I ever had.

Emancipate yourself from mental slavery.

Ah boy, bring me the Breeze.

The black bird whistles in the tree above,

looking down at white clothes in blue water.

Fowls cackle, waiting for their feed.

Boy, bring me a pack of Blue.

The enticing smell of breadfruit roasting on a bonfire,

plantains frying on a coal pot.

The yachts dance across the vista.

Boy, bring me a glass of water.

*Adonal Foyle*

The sun dips behind the ocean.

She spills the water from the tub

lifting her eyes to the heavens.

As if to say where has the day gone?

## RUNNING

One by one I pass them

on the dirt paved road

running home from school

sweat dripping from my face

drenching my khaki uniform.

The sun peels my skin.

I keep on running.

Even the searing comments from friends

could not stop me.

"Hey sissy, faggot, mama's boy."

I ignore them.

Almost home, I run to Granny

standing in the distance, the

sun descending behind her

into the reflecting sea, hands

behind her back, clanging wire

*Adonal Foyle*

bracelets, twisted white head tie

thick white glasses covering cast

eyes.

I keep running.

My eyes focus on a blank face.

I don't see the whip grasped tightly,

her anger needs no reason,

Echoes smack across my face.

She grabs my escape.

I run no more.

## QUESTIONS

How do you know when to plant?

When the moon gets big like a pumpkin

and the clouds get ugly like your big nose.

And if the rain don't come?

Then we will call it, with drums

and dancing at the cross street.

And if it still don't come?

We'll go to church and pray for downpours,

heavenly father never gives us more than we can bear.

And if he forgets to turn on the faucet?

*Adonal Foyle*

We kill a goat, shed its blood and prepare an offering

to those gone before us and to the good Lord,

beseeching his mercy.

Suppose after all this no rain come?

Better eat up then.

We might need you for lunch

one of these days if things get tough.

## SHE SAID

Them see bird wine.

Them say it's sweetness.

Reality is but an illusion.

*Adonal Foyle*

## BEFORE THEY THROW YOU IN THE GROUND

The intoxicating rhythm of the

steel pan feeds their zeal.

They sing to rhythm of Dan Sandy's banjo

and Gabriel with his African drum.

Death they say is the beginning.

They wine their bompsie to the ground

joke of her wickedness,

Bacardi and Sunset, coconut water,

a splash of lime squash made them delirious.

Salt fish and bakes move center front.

Death they say is not the end.

The tambourines shake to the lyrics

of Banana Man and they tell Nancy stories

that nail you to your chair.

Then they pass my small trembling frame over her coffin and under it.

Death I say is a scary thing.

## MAYPOLE DANCING

My aunt Islar likes the regatta

more than fighting to lead church song.

But she wanted only one event.

She was not interested in the egg and spoon,

the boat races, the queen show,

not even the calypso show.

She was 81 and skilled like a matador.

A solitary pole stands proud

with bright multi-colored strings

descending from its apex.

They drop like shimmering snow in the island sun.

She wears the blue flower dress

that her good child got her.

*Adonal Foyle*

Sandy sound the drum.

They circle the pole like a pack of wild animals,

ready to pounce on their prey.

They glide forward, as if to salute,

then the drummers let loose

like my neighbor's bad dog chasing

me from the mango tree.

Auntie Islar's string was bright orange.

They heed the call of the drum.

They weave a net so tight

the spider web in my dirty room

had nothing on them

crossing, ducking, spinning.

A tyro's mistake was greeted with a growl

or a swing of her hips,

but by the end of the dance though bruised

everyone will know how to dance the May Pole.

My Aunt's favorite regatta event.

## DRY SEASON

Just as the sun belches night

and falls into a slumber,

villagers crawl from every

crevice of the island.

From Clifton, Ashton,

Bigsand, Murray,

Forthhill, Bighill,

Jerome, Downson,

Point-look-out,

Valley, Waterbreak,

Bloodybay,

Bush, Saltpond,

Goathill.

Catcalls of the drum beckon

them to the crossroad,

with lanterns and torches,

with cloth wrapped

around their foreheads,

*Adonal Foyle*

with gunslingers and

sunflashes on their feet.

A Caribbean fruit bowl,

unity unbending.

They form a circle.

At its center two cloth pieces cross each other,

begging for someone

to take the challenge.

The drummers beat leather

until their hands bleed,

calling to the rain god,

begging for rain.

Two ladies heed the drum,

grab the cloth,

weaving it through the air,

shouting,

"Zumbanaty de eh noty de en not the bubani."

## ISLAND WITCH

She claims it comes like a thief in dead of night,

to suck your blood and leave you thin and dry.

It screams and sighs until the break of light,

the blazing fire cuts the ominous sky.

It passes through the tiniest of cracks,

a bolted door or keyhole is no match.

To stop it one must find its hidden tracks.

Its shredded skin will be the hunter's catch.

With salt and pepper stain the hunter's prey,

to burn and burn will be its deadly fate.

And it must turn towards the morning rays,

the zephyr pulls the sun onto the lake.

The soucouyant parades the tarry sky,

as trembling in my childhood bed, I lie.

*Adonal Foyle*

## DAMN SUN

Before I am ready, the sun climbs through

the crevices of the door and settles on my eyes.

I can smell the morning glory

scuffling with balsam tea boiling on the fire,

and when I open the door I taste the sea salt

upon my lips. The chirping of the doctor bird.

She sings, Rock of Ages cleft for me,

let me hide myself in thee.

The guava tree sways, stirred repeatedly

by the breeze climbing gently off the ocean.

Then warplanes explode across the sky

as I seek a futile refuge beneath my bed.

The United States invades Grenada.

My world becomes a battleground.

Who knows how these things get started

but I would like to volunteer a few guesses,

*When the Ball is Laid to Rest*

The evil Grenadian with communist intent
or Reagan social policies that's not worth a cent.

Whatever the excuse the masses accept,
the island was leveled with fighter jets.

Bishop and them were put in jail
do you know no one accepted their bail?

They went to the fort in handcuffs
and were shot in the head without much fuss.

Now I am not blaming the US for the deed
that would be most unfortunate indeed.

Was it Castro's manipulative assistant
the Grenadian cunning ploy of resistance?

Charles draws the US a backdoor map
Manley's made sure there was no gap.

Coard was the man who started the war
Reagan wanted a sure victory from afar.

*Adonal Foyle*

## SLIDING IN COPPER POT

Placid turned a turtle

on the midnight beach.

We parked in his yard the next morning,

like chicken hawks waiting

to devour my grandmother's

newborn chicks.

Riding in turtle shell down grassy hills,

sledding right back into the sea,

much faster than my mother's copper pot.

Three boys in a turtle shell racing to the sea.

## WE TOO CAN BUILD COMPUTER CHIPS

No one tills the soil,

such proud people,

keepers of the land.

Bags of peanuts,

mountains of peas,

oceans of corn,

red sweet potatoes,

scarecrows with

big straw hats.

Fishermen's gum boats,

pulled to the shore,

hidden in the shade

of the Tackaberry.

Now we scrub,

white man's floor,

from seven to four,

for pennies.

*Adonal Foyle*

My beaches

sold to strangers,

my gardens

golf courses with tiny carts.

Farmers, fishermen, are

independent contractors, waiters,

laundry specialists,

toilet engineers.

What will we do,

when the beaches are

gone?

Damn you beautiful beaches,

I curse the day you were born.

You bought the tourists,

charmed them with your Caribbean breeze,

golden sand,

diamond sparkling water.

*When the Ball is Laid to Rest*

I am no hater of tourism

nor of Green gold.

But must we live a hurricane

away from poverty?

My people,

turn the banana to drinks,

make tourism work

for our children.

We beat colonization,

even slavery.

We are smart.

Me want Doctors,

Professors,

Engineers,

Scientists.

Me want education man.

*Adonal Foyle*
# SWEET CHANT

I smell your rotten breast

before seeing your shriveled face

hearing your silent scream,

groans and unanswered pleas.

The gaping hole in your breast

can fit a basketball

with oozing fluid that

becomes your swimming pool.

So many years of love

and hatred we shared.

How ungrateful I've become

refusing to honor a simple wish.

How hard could it be to put

a pillow over your face,

empty life from an empty shell

forcing your pills down your throat.

*When the Ball is Laid to Rest*

Choking you to silence.

But I stand paralyzed

a desperate plea until

the sweet chant

of inevitability beckons you

to the brink.

A pungent longing radiates your

countenance.

*Adonal Foyle*
## REMBEMBERING HER

And like a terrible hurricane silencing a once rowdy island,

or the fire that burns the soul in Gomorrah,

the storyteller's chair sits vacant,

a shawl across the back.

Her hoe no longer ploughs the loamy soil.

A lady climbing Manny Hill,

white ECFM flour bag

filled with peanuts and potatoes

balanced on her head,

disappears into the rays of the

steamy Caribbean sun.

Like serenades knocking on your door

capturing your air and escaping into the

cover of night, she gone.

Vanished the dancing and singing to bring in the morning.

The crooked eyes close one last time.

*When the Ball is Laid to Rest*

I sit in the plum tree

waiting for a glimpse

of your sunburnt face.

But all I can see is

memory.

*Adonal Foyle*

## A PLACE OF MYSTERY

Of time and place without a name

narrow paths and winding roads,

of secrets old and filled with shame,

a falling star that no man hoards.

If I sound foolish, cold and bleak,

judge me not with hate or scorn,

pity me for I fear what I seek,

unleash the raging passions born.

How many went to that raw place?

Where air balls and injuries roam.

Even a child must run this race,

to conquer thee, the masses moan.

I end this query with shame and fear

but look, there, nearer to the clear...

## REMEMBERING THE PAST

I miss the cocks that shout out loud

arise, arise you wretched sloth

the day has dawned and passed by

dragging night's drape across the sky.

I miss the beach, the sand that's pure

the water that makes the land secure.

Its reef, a quilt with blinding hues

adorn the painted life below.

I miss the pain I ever hate

those whips, those ropes, those haunting palms

one does not only love the good

but grows accustomed to the bad.

I miss my cow and donkey too

my crazy sheep and maggar goats.

They were my friends and confidants

though always mute, they seemed to know.

*Adonal Foyle*

I miss the face of those trusted few

whose love was but a weakness fought.

I love them all and hate them too

for they are blind to history.

# Pick and Roll

*The game of basketball has been everything to me. My place of refuge, place I've always gone where I needed comfort and peace. It's been the site of intense pain and the most intense feelings of joy and satisfaction.*
*It's a relationship that has evolved over time, given me the greatest respect and love for the game.*

                      Michael
                      Jordan

*Adonal Foyle*

## LOSING

Naked, folded up under the steaming shower

my ass vibrating

from the water bouncing off the hard floor.

Clutching my hairy face,

I watch bodies enter and leave,

seeing no faces,

only black and white muscled legs,

fungus feet, broken toenails.

The water stones my aching body.

My fog veiled eyes turn from theirs,

stare down at the towel soaking in the

water on the floor.

I try to catch my tears,

but they are indistinguishable from the hard dry water.

I count 244 tiles covering the mildewed floor.

## AIR BALL

And it rolls off my figures like rain

dancing through the forest leaves.

It is seamless.

But it misses, catching no iron.

At home, silence envelopes the arena.

Then a quiet rumble slips through the crowd.

On the road the fans erupt,

booing, laughing, clapping, hissing.


I quiet my soul.

You got me.

But I will never let you know.

I play on…

*Adonal Foyle*

## COURT AT NIGHT

I never knew you slept.

Nightly silence holds you close.

Quiet nets dangle, waiting for

tomorrow's pleasures.

Your repellent floor defines your origin.

Smell of burnt rubber,

lingers like a skunk marking its territory.

Sleep, my raging warrior,

for today you got the best of me.

## JUST BUSINESS

A vacant locker,

a solitary jersey hanging lifelessly,

yesterday's sweat.

A pair of used Nikes like a fallen warrior.

No one mourns his death.

Life goes on as usual,

or maybe they cry silently

as they run the pick and roll for the hundredth time.

A loss that becomes another's security.

Like a village besieged by a plague

taking victims one after another,

a hovering soul that no one talks about.

A dirty secret buried in shame.

"Where is number 13?"

"Cut!"

*Adonal Foyle*

## DRUMMING THE WARRIORS BACK TO LIFE

You voodoo gods of Caribbean isles,

I call to you across the miles,

Come with me to the Oakland shores,

bring ancestral potions mixed with cloves,

suffused with lavender, garlic, balsamic bliss,

let's burn these demons with a hiss,

and drive them through the valley mist.

Follow me to the House of Game,

to rid this den of its mask of shame.

Shake your head and beat your chest,

burn your candles in distress,

spill water of religious lore,

blood of hen in corners four,

crash your cymbals in the air,

mix the earwax with a hair.

For who knows the secrets of this cave,

of men whose lives have not been saved?

We splatter like rain on an old tin roof

*When the Ball is Laid to Rest*

and in a moment become aloof.

Losing makes a man go sick,

teach us how to seek the wick.

Broken ornaments, we are cast aside,

seemingly as if we'd died.

Don't tell me that we lack the skills,

to give the people their dose of thrills,

the Raiders win, the A's do too,

what more must our poor Warriors do?

Dance to the beat of this here drum,

the voodoo man to town has come,

he moans, he groans, his spells are cast,

echoes of our ancient past,

hear we, ye ghosts of evil intent,

vanish! Warriors, embrace content.

And so we glide from goal to goal,

our fertile future to unfold.

*Adonal Foyle*
## WARRIOR OF THE BAY

How do I measure the heart of a man,

when that man sees his

contribution as simply doing his part?

Many traverse the hardwood floor, but few bend it to their will.

Sharp to the very end,

greatness is not about speaking of greatness …

but allowing your adversaries to boast of your ferocity and elegance.

When your ball was laid to rest, you taught us how to make

the world your playground.

Unafraid to journey into the unknown, donning an apron and

cooking the famous ribs we still talk about, becoming the

man to tell the tales of hoop heaven to a new generation of

Dub Nation faithfuls.

Why must he go, I ask.

He is the best of us.

Who will show us the path of greatness paved with such humility?

*When the Ball is Laid to Rest*

He was a tower with the heart of an angel.
In the midst of great chatter he walked with dignity, allowing history to come to its own conclusion.

Our friend has gone to sleep, but the quilt of excellence that hangs in our collective memory will forever be the template of his immortality.

I learned many lessons from this gentle giant, but no more profound than in the midst of the chaos, hold firm to your optimism and infect the skeptics with hope.

Our dear friend has gone to rest, but how many like him can say I was here, and left an indelible mark on every soul I encountered on this road called life?

Fear not.
You will have dinner with the angels tonight.
But know that the lesson is learned.

For I have your eternal optimism held close to my heart.
Sleep well until we meet again
Warrior of the Bay.

*Adonal Foyle*

## LOVE SONG TO A GAME

How should I tell thee goodbye?

What can you say about a love affair

to rival that of Romeo & Juliet?

This is not just some melancholy ode

to a hackneyed love of mortals.

I found our love deep in the entrails of the Caribbean Sea.

Love that swept me to a land where our embrace became mythical.

You showed me a world that few have dreamt of.

Colgate's golden steeple,

a sojourn where ancient teachings flooded my mind.

There in the Chenango Valley

where 13 sang my soul to flight,

basketball laid siege to my soul.

I do not cry for the passing of our love

for it stands radiant,

while my brittle bones crumble through swift time.

I have known you by so many faces.

Its only truth lies in the understanding it will all end.

*When the Ball is Laid to Rest*

I will spend my end of days recalling.

You have infected many

with the allure of riches and black gold.

But I am not angry with you my love.

For to a boy who was lost in the bosom of nothing,

you gave hope and home.

Like the flickering of a light we come and go

without much fuss.

So I leave you to fend off seekers,

hoping they too will cherish your unyielding countenance.

As for me, I will forever live in the glare

of your loving embrace.

From time to time I hope you will look in on this pitiful fool.

I will miss brothers of a quilt struggling with burning lights.

I offer advice, pierce beyond the glaring lights,

and see the faces behind the wall.

Don't be fooled by the magicians' nimble fingers,

for this is a life with mirrors and screens.

*Adonal Foyle*

Its only truth lies in the understanding it will all end.

The sound I will take home

is the symphony of thousands of screaming friends.

Warriors, Magic and yes, Memphis too,

I sing you praise, hope, blessings.

Flowing from a boy's songs of thanks

to you and you and you, to all I knew.

Please stay my "immortal love."

# *POLITICS*

*There comes a time when one must take a position that is neither safe, nor politic, nor popular, but he must take it because conscience tells him it is right.*

Martin Luther King Jr.

*Adonal Foyle*

## BENEATH THE WAVING FLAG

Beneath the waving flag

the ground feels no rain,

the earth remains the same

the withering plant finally dies.

Beneath the waving flag

everyone sings the hymn of conformity,

dialogue locked in the coffin of fear

feet trampled in unison and contempt.

Beneath the waving flag

no one can hear me scream,

I cannot see the sun

faces hidden in zealousness.

Beneath the waving flag

stupidity is called patriotism,

greed and revenge moral codes

terrorism a mad man's reprieve.

*When the Ball is Laid to Rest*

Beneath the waving flag

Enron becomes a memory,

questions are the enemy

fear our justifiable gift.

Beneath the waving flag

my freedom borrowed,

we become blind AlQuedans

zealousness without moderation.

Beneath the waving flag

I cried for dead victims across the world,

I cried for 9-11

I cried for clarity of leaders.

Beneath the waving flag

We did not rage when unmanned

planes killed Americans

without due process.

*Adonal Foyle*

Beneath the waving flag

Barbara Lee vilified

for her conscientious votes.

Beneath the waving flag

killing their innocence,

collateral damage and ours

unspeakable horror and murder?

Beneath the waving flag

I am afraid to sign this poem.

Beneath the waving flag

I cannot breathe.

## THE KING OF HIS TIME

The King.

Prizefighter refusing to raise his gloves,

inflicting a moral whipping.

Like a kid he dares the bully to take a punch,

from his wounds the blood of love poured.

His tears quenched the thirst of millions,

his religion was a beacon on uncharted waters,

his imprisonment the hope of his children,

his death the price for our freedom.

Love was the dagger of his salvation.

A matador waving his cape

before a raging bull,

forcing it into submission,

despite its sharpened horns.

*Adonal Foyle*

## GLORY

They run into the muzzle of the cannons

like a relay team,

as one drops dead another grabs the banner of courage

and charges.

From the heads of fallen warriors

they rise.

Clambering with the conviction of those old Negro spirituals,

a procession of death,

bomb-covered night,

they fall to their deaths like loyal knights

for a cause they make their own.

Like the mountain-climbing rhythm of Carl's Carmina,

to the top of Fort Wagner they ascend,

and fall like Shakespeare's tragic heroes.

# A LOVE STORY

*The power of a glance has been so much abused in love stories that it has come to be disbelieved. Few people daresay nowadays that two beings have fallen in love because they have looked at each other. Yet that is the way love begins, and only that way.*

Victor Hugo

*Adonal Foyle*
# BREAKFAST AT CHOWS

The steady gaze in her direction

as if to capture every lost memory.

The look of love that showers your face

as you fixed the napkin on her lap

reminding her to blow her hot tea before sipping.

You cut her blueberry pancake into bite size pieces.

She let you without complaining.

She is used to you fussing over her.

Unexpected whispers followed by bouts of giggles.

She chews in a slow monotonous rhythm

and you clean her mouth with glee.

Your patience annoys me.

Sewing a barely visible cloth resting gently on her lap.

As I abandon my table I inadvertently discover

a smile on my face.

I fell in love with two women at a table.

## WANING SANITY

A sleeping smile shatters a million contradictions.

Bright darkness envelops my waning sanity and

a yearning hatred corrodes the nightly stench.

Sleep bids adieu to the lucid grasp

and escapes to the torrent of stupidity,

where right and wrong move to the unbiased beat of dreaming.

A stolen gaze into the uncanny stream reveals longing and loathing.

Truth is an ugly figure camouflaged with the linen of time.

Sleeping ignorance disrobes a million contradictions.

She who carries the torch of justice,

bends the stubborn mule by forcing it to regurgitate

the fangs of an elusive darkness.

She is as unyielding as she is conscientious.

*Adonal Foyle*

## NIGHT AND DAY: A LOVE POEM

Fear not ghost of darkness,

master of night's realm,

morning's light will not dowse

your fiery midnight passion,

locked in my bosom of eternal touch.

Dagger of day pierces your trembling inclination,

burnishing you with ubiquitous fear of unnatural longing.

A camellia of mundane tranquility,

serpentines through a chorus

of unexplored betrayal, of untested feelings.

How you move through night's shade,

with the nobility of kingly privileges,

steps leaving undeniable prints of passage.

Lestat[1] must have taught you how to rule

the dark heaven of your true calling.

---

[1] The Vampire Lestat (1985) is a vampire novel by Anne Rice, and the second in her Vampire Chronicles, following *Interview with the Vampire*.

Concealed jealousy waters a sanguine journey,

of unreachable hope lost in night and day.

Man's path chokes with life's grand design.

Looting animals pray for Shakespearean fall.

Slivers of mistrust precipitate the fall.

Nature's truth undeniable,

imposing presence trapped by day's glaring rays.

We were naked in the dawn of possibilities

morning's gloom threatened last night's hopeful union.

Wretched day be gone,

you belch poison upon my face.

You ghost, who walks night's corner and midday's roads,

proudly displaying a band

that masks the dual truth of oneness,

I am savagely in awe.

Day walker - night stalker

lives an indistinguishable truth,

with a simplistic need of survival.

*Adonal Foyle*

Must not day abandon its heightened chord of war,

and walk in the slippers of 'live and let live?'

Night, who clutches our secrets,

allows mortals a sojourn

from morning sadness and midday blues.

## LOVE ON A TRAIN

*London, Kings Cross*

To watch a face that says so much,

yet utters not a word to thee,

as though another language is at hand,

at arm's length, "Touch not."

To live with an inadvertent glance, a secret stare,

a moving train is easier caught.

To sit across and write what should be spoken in embrace,

to rip your clothes, proclaiming to the world

I have found the one.

*Stevenage*

But wait, she does not love in return,

she feels no fire, no sudden palpitation,

no sickness, no bolt of lightning.

Thus I must cage cupid and store him in a safe place

to keep him from obvious harm.

*Adonal Foyle*

*Peterborough*

Stranded on our way to Scotland,

pacing up and down the platform,

blue jeans, brown sandals, and a blue jacket.

Should I scream at the top of my voice my love for her?

Dooming my chances and destroying the placid ambiance?

How can one stay so silent?

Watching with such passion,

open pastures, green trees,

grazing sheep and stupid cows?

What is the way into a pin vault?

There must be a code,

Or shall I blow it up?

A chill on the platform,

the train has been terminated.

I smell remorse tainting the evening sky,

the sun admits defeat and dies to be reborn.

*When the Ball is Laid to Rest*

Losing my seat on the next train,

I must content myself with sitting behind her,

barely glimpsing the top of her head.

My legs a conductor's hazard,

shall I put them in my mouth?

A storm is brewing,

ugly dark clouds hang ominously,

in front of the train.

I speed through them,

moving into danger without fear,

Man of La Mancha.

My second cup of coffee,

my third cup of tea,

my fourth drink of water,

my final fruit candy.

*Adonal Foyle*

*Newark North Gate*

I will turn my world upside down for you if you but ask,

I would walk the ends of the earth

to get a blade of grass that she wanted.

How foolish can a man be?

I will give up my morality at her command.

What the hell am I writing?

Pure rubbish.

I sit and write bad poetry in the hills of Scotland.

I look out from Carlton Hill and I am happy

watching gothic structures and baroque buildings

painting the valley below.

Will somebody put this fool out of his misery?

Maybe I am a little train sick.

Oh that's it.

No it's not.

*When the Ball is Laid to Rest*

I was fine yesterday when we walked the streets of London

climbing up on a lion's back to show my spunk.

I sit in beautiful theaters marveling at talent,

*The Birthday Party, The Three Sisters, Miss Saigon,*

and memorable sights,

the Tower of London,

Globe Theater,

Mr. Ben guarding the harbor,

The Castle afloat on water.

To feel history move through you,

enjoying its pleasures and its horrors.


How timid she looks standing beside the Guard.

As the gadfly with a camera urges her to get closer,

how red her face becomes - such sweet hatred,

walking to unknown places to ease a fearful mind.

*Adonal Foyle*

*Berwick Upon-Tweed*

Her face in the reflecting glass,

so pretty, not conventional prettiness,

she has that too,

but much more,

mystery and simplicity.

A smile, a thought,

then a pensive gaze beyond the glass of the train.

I can feel her face,

it speaks to me,

it sings to me,

but I cannot understand the words or lyrics.

Norma Desmond where are you?

I think she is happy.

*When the Ball is Laid to Rest*

She has worn that smile for ten minutes now,

she loves the child reading in front of her,

she loves what she sees beyond the train,

she loves the freedom of the open air,

don't stop, what else does she love?

Please don't stop, what else does she love?

She takes a picture,

definitely she loves the view.

# GLOSSORY OF CARIBBEAN TERMS

**Bakes**: Fresh baked small bun made from flour, baking soda or yeast.

**Blue**: A kind of detergent that is blue in color and is used to soak white clothes in order to regain their color.

**Breadfruit:** It is a kind of fruit that you eat. The national dish of St. Vincent and the Grenadines that was brought to the island by Captain Bligh.

**Breeze**: A detergent that is used for washing clothes.

**Bompsie**: Your ass (bottom).

**Calypso**: A kind of music. The musician sings about issues affecting their community and country.

**Carta**: A piece of cloth wrapped in circles and is placed under heavy load on a person's head.

**Cashee**: A cactus with prickers that bear edible fruits.

**Chilibibby**: Popcorn ground in a mill to a fine consistency. It is then eaten with sugar.

**Coal Pot**: A round, movable fireplace that people cook on especially when it rains. A cooking device using charcoal, consisting of a raised iron bowl and a central grid.

**Conch**: Any of various tropical mollusks having a large spiral shell with a flared opening.

**Comess**: Gossip.

**Dub**: A genre of music born out of reggae music in the 1960's. In many respects, it became a sub-genre of reggae.

**Duckner**: A corn made food cooked wrapped in banana leaves.

**Fete**: A party!

**Green Gold**: Another name for banana once referred to as the lifeblood of the Caribbean.

**Jabless**: A kind of dead spirit that tends to be meaner than the jumbi.

**Jacks**: A kind of fish that fishermen catch in large quantities with a net. They travel in schools.

**Jubay**: Part of a Carnival celebration.

**Jumbie, Jumbi, or Jumby**: A ghost.

**Jumbi Table**: A table with many different foods set up for the spirits to eat from. Usually as an offering.

**Lambi**: A conch. A snail like creature that lives in the sea in a shell. It is also the name of my uncle because he built a restaurant out of conch shells.

**Lime Squash**: Another name for lemonade.

**Mass**: This is another name for carnival. It originates from masquerade. The art of dressing up into costumes for the purpose of a celebration.

**Maggar**: Skinny.

**Maypole dancing**: Weaving strings around a pole while music is playing. A maypole is a tall wooden pole erected as a part of various European folk festivals, particularly in the Caribbean on May Day.

**Nancy stories**: Very popular in terms of Caribbean story telling, and a direct transfer from West Africa to the Caribbean.

**Netball**: A game very much like basketball except it is predominately played by women and there is no dribbling. The ball is advanced by passing and shooting through a small ring.

**Nine Morning**: Nine days of dancing before Christmas.

**Reggae**: A kind of music made famous by Bob Marley and the Wailers.

**Sankathrow**: A soup with a little of everything. It is called the "poor man brew" because whatever food scraps you have available, you throw into it—like Jambalaya.

**Soca**: A kind of music made famous by Trinidad and Tobago.

**Socouyant**: They are equivalent to witches.

**Soursop**: A fruit with a fleshy milky-like consistency.

**Souse**: A soup made with pig feet.

**Sunset**: A strong kind of coconut rum with a proof of over 80.

**Tambran (tamarind) balls:** A fruit that is harvested and blended with sugar has a sweet and sour taste.

**Tackaberry Tree**: A tree that bears a fruit that is a great adhesive.

**Wine**: To dance provocatively.

**Wilkes**: A small sea creature that sticks to the rocks.

**Wongoo**: A food made entirely of corn. America will call it polenta.

# ABOUT THE AUTHOR

Adonal Foyle played 13 seasons in the NBA: 10 with the Golden State Warriors, three with the Orlando Magic and one game with the Memphis Grizzlies. After hanging up his jersey, he served two seasons as the Director of Player Programs for the Orlando Magic.

Adonal graduated magna cum laude from Colgate University with a degree in history. He earned his master's degree in sports psychology (which he began during his NBA career), from John F. Kennedy University in Pleasant Hill, California. His master's thesis, for which he interviewed numerous colleagues, was an in-depth study into the life changes experienced by NBA players upon retirement.

Adonal is also the Founder & President of two non-profit organizations. His Kerosene Lamp Foundation empowers at-risk youths through athletics & academics camps, mentorship, and literacy initiatives. His other non-profit, Democracy Matters, encourages young people to get involved in the political system and let their voices be heard.

Adonal has received numerous honors, including induction into the World Sports Humanitarian Hall of Fame and the CoSIDA Academic All-America Hall of Fame, appointment as Goodwill Ambassador of St. Vincent & the Grenadines, NBA Players Association Community Contribution All-Star Award and Social Change Agent (Greenlining Institute).

In his spare time, Adonal enjoys reading, wine-tasting, playing racquetball, traveling and writing poetry.

**Contact the Author**

www.AdonalFoyle.com

www.FoyleConsulting.com

Twitter.com/afoyle3131

Facebook.com/FoylesForum

*When the Ball is Laid to Rest*